C 1

COMMERCIAL AIRPLANES

The new compact study guide and identifier

IDENTIFYING

i

COMMERCIAL
AIRPLANES

The new compact study guide and identifier

David Lee

CHARTWELL
BOOKS, INC.

A QUINTET BOOK

Published by **Chartwell Books**
A Division of **Book Sales, Inc.**
114, Northfield Avenue
Edison, New Jersey 08837

This edition produced for sale in the U.S.A., its territories and
dependencies only.

ISBN 0-7858-1019-6

This book was designed and produced by
Quintet Publishing Limited
6 Blundell Street
London N7 9BH

Creative Director: Richard Dewing
Art Director: Lucy Parissi
Designer: TT Designs
Project Editor: Keith Ryan
Editor: Andrew Armitage
Illustrator: Tony Townsend

Photography courtesy of:
Bombardier Regional Aircraft pp 2, 30, 43, 53; Airbus Industrie pp
6, 8, 10, 45, 46, 47, 48, 64; Saab Aircraft International pp 7, 24,
25; Boeing pp 9, 49, 50, 51, 60, 61, 65, 66, 67, 78; Raytheon
Aircraft Company p 12; Gerry Manning pp 13 (top), 16, 17, 20, 22,
23, 35, 39, 40, 42, 52, 54, 57, 58, 59, 62, 63, 68, 69, 72, 73;
British Aerospace ATM pp 13 (bottom), 14, 15, 70, 76; Embraer pp
18, 19, 55, 77; Aero International (Regional) pp 26, 27; CASA pp
28, 29; Fairchild Dormier (Dormier Luftfahrt GmbH) pp 31, 32, 33;
Jersey European Airways pp 34, 38; British Airways pp 36, 37, 75;
Lockheed Martin Corporation pp 40, 58; British World Airways p 41;
HeavyLift Cargo Airlines pp 44, 71; KLM Royal Dutch Airlines
(Capital Photos) p 56

Typeset in Great Britain by
Central Southern Typesetters, Eastbourne
Manufactured in Singapore by Eray Scan Ltd
Printed in Singapore by Star Standard Industries (Pte) Ltd

I wish to express my thanks to two special women:
Linda Maxwell Mason for converting the manuscript into a
form acceptable to my publishers! Jeannie, my wife, for her support,
love, and advice.

CONTENTS

INTRODUCTION		**6**
COMMERCIAL AVIATION REVIEW		**8**
WHAT OF THE FUTURE?		**9**
HOW TO USE THIS BOOK		**10**
INTERNATIONAL REGISTRATION PREFIX		**11**
SECTION A	**TWO PROPELLER ENGINES – LOW WING**	**12**
SECTION B	**TWO PROPELLER ENGINES – HIGH WING**	**26**
SECTION C	**FOUR PROPELLER ENGINES – LOW WING**	**39**
SECTION D	**FOUR PROPELLER ENGINES – HIGH WING**	**42**
SECTION E	**TWO JET ENGINES – LOW WING**	**45**
SECTION F	**TWO JET ENGINES – TAIL-MOUNTED**	**53**
SECTION G	**THREE JET ENGINES – LOW WING AND TAIL-MOUNTED**	**58**
SECTION H	**THREE JET ENGINES – TAIL-MOUNTED**	**60**
SECTION I	**FOUR JET ENGINES – LOW WING**	**64**
SECTION J	**FOUR JET ENGINES – HIGH WING**	**70**
SECTION K	**FOUR JET ENGINES – TAIL-MOUNTED**	**72**
SECTION L	**FOUR JET ENGINES – DELTA**	**74**
APPENDIX – AERO ENGINES		**75**
BIBLIOGRAPHY & Other Recommended Reference Sources		**79**

INTRODUCTION

In just one generation, air travel has been transformed from being the sole prerogative of the rich, to being available to all. Foremost among the many technical advances that have helped create this transport revolution has been the development of the jet engine. Of the many important aircraft two, more than any others, have created the present air-travel industry – both Boeing designs: the 707 and unique 747. This book will help you identify these renowned aircraft and the many others to be seen at airports, large and small, throughout the world.

If you are new to the study of civil aviation, you will be rewarded by an insight into the infinitely fascinating world of commercial aircraft. Unlike military machines, which tend to have uniform, standardized color schemes, civil airliners carry an endless variety of colorful liveries as each airline and operator seeks to promote its own business. Their aircraft are their most prominent and popular method of advertising.

At any international airport, you may find commercial aircraft from every corner of the world. There are nearly 500 operators registered in over 150 countries and the majority fly international routes on either scheduled or charter services. Identifying the aircraft, its operator, and country of origin is all part of the excitement of watching civil aviation in action.

SELECTION OF AIRCRAFT

The aircraft illustrated are restricted to those involved in the commercial carrying of passengers or freight. Therefore specialist business/corporate aircraft and those in the general aviation sector are excluded. Most of the chosen aircraft are in full production and in widespread international use. Some are, however, long out of production and their numbers are dwindling, for example the Vickers Viscount and the Douglas DC-4/6/7 series. Even if they are few in number, they remain in commercial service and their importance to the development of civil aviation fully justifies their inclusion. Other designs are relatively new and are only just entering service in, as yet, limited numbers. Examples include the Tupolev TU-204 and the Airtech CN-235. Whether or not their full potential will be rewarded by large-scale orders – only time will tell.

COMMERCIAL AVIATION REVIEW

The past dozen or so years have seen dramatic changes in commercial aviation, none more so than in the former Soviet Union following the collapse of communist rule.

Under the Soviet system, a civil aircraft manufacturer had, in effect, one customer – the national airline, Aeroflot. Following approval to build a particular aircraft, the manufacturer was virtually guaranteed a long production run, almost irrespective of the commercial viability of the design. Sales abroad were virtually restricted to fellow communist nations. That was all swept away with the fall of communism.

The former Aeroflot fragmented into many dozens of separate commercial operators with unfamiliar names, such as Aerokuznetsk, Domodedovo Airlines, Sakhaavia, and Turkmenistan Air. Aeroflot still exists as Aeroflot Russian International Airlines but is a tiny remnant of its former size. Russian and Ukrainian airplane manufacturers now have to produce commercial aircraft fully competitive with their Western counterparts. The need to sell their products in the West has led to the installation of Western aero-engines in versions of aircraft such as Tupolev TU-204 and Ilyushin IL-114.

In Western commercial aviation, it has been deregulation in Europe and the United States of America that has produced the most profound changes. A major consequence in the USA has been the disappearance of large well-established airlines such as Pan-American, Eastern Airlines, and Braniff and the emergence of low-cost airlines. One of the pioneers of this movement – Valujet – has, following a disastrous accident, recently merged with AirTran Airways to form AirTran Airlines.

In Europe, the formerly nationalized British Airways has, under privatization, been strengthened and is now a major world airline. Other smaller national European airlines are seeking partners in order to compete. As in the United States low-cost airlines have been formed and their impact is such that British Airways have launched their own budget airline, named "GO".

Manufacture of the large international airliners is dominated by Boeing but with Airbus Industrie now providing serious competition. The once dominant Douglas – later McDonnell Douglas – is now part of the Boeing group.

Production of the smaller regional and commuter airliners is undertaken by a number of different manufacturers and it is this field that new companies such as IPTN of Indonesia have emerged.

WHAT OF THE FUTURE?

The escalating cost of designing and building the major international airliners is already beyond the financial capabilities of an individual company (with the possible exception of Boeing) and even of individual nations. The trend toward international companies typified by the Airbus Industrie consortium and the sharing of development costs as in the SAAB 2000 is certain to accelerate.

Planning for a new, very large airliner to replace and/or supplement the Boeing 747 has been underway by Boeing and Airbus Industrie for more than five years. The Airbus design is provisionally called the A3XX and is expected to carry up to 990 passengers on two decks. Powered by four engines in the 75,000 lbst (334 kN)-thrust class, the design would have a maximum range of 8,600 miles (13,900k m). It is, however, very unlikely that Airbus Industrie will go ahead with production alone. As it will be looking for risk-sharing partners, it is not impossible that Boeing and Airbus could jointly build a VLCT (Very large Commercial Transport) in the twenty-first century.

If the development of a VLCT is a commercial risk, it pales into insignificance when compared with the cost of producing a replacement for Concorde. Both the American competitors of the late 1960s, the Boeing 2707 and the Lockheed L-2000, were stillborn with only a full-scale Boeing mock-up surviving in a theme park. Design studies of potential SSTs (Supersonic Transports) appear at regular intervals but fail to achieve formal status. However, one example of the Russian Tupolev TU-144 supersonic airliner has been returned to flying status, with American funding, to carry out research into supersonic flight on behalf of the United States. Environmental problems are likely to be the major obstacle that any future SST will have to overcome. Noise, pollution, the ozone layer, and especially the impact of the sonic boom are likely to be most pressing environmental issues.

HOW TO USE THIS BOOK

To help you to identify a specific commercial aircraft, this book is divided into 12 sections (A to L). Each section contains aircraft with the same configuration in respect to means of propulsion (propeller or jet), location and number of engines, and the position of the wing on the fuselage.In addition, icons and silhouettes have been included to help illustrate these key features.

The illustrations are as follows:

- **Engine propulsion: Propeller or Jet.**
  Note that "shp" means shaft horsepower and "lbst" means pounds static thrust. They are also expressed in kilowatts (kW) and kilonewtons (kN) respectively.
- **Number of engines: Two, Three or Four.**
  This is indicated at the top right corner of these icons.

- **Engine position: On the wing, near the tail or on the wing and near the tail.**

- **Wing position: High on the fuselage or low on the fuselage.**

The silhouettes represent the approximate view of an airplane in any given category, as viewed from the side and the front. This will help you pick out the key identifying features with greater ease whether passing overhead or sitting between flights on the airport tarmac.

Identification

Having reached the correct section, you may at first – especially if you are new to the art of recognizing aircraft – find that they still tend to look the same. This is inevitable, since similar technical requirements tend to produce similar technical solutions. There also tend to be "fashions" in aircraft designs – in the 1960s it was for rear-engined airliners, recently it is for having two very large engines – one on each wing. By close study of the photographs and by comparing the technical data, you should find that the variations between the different types of aircraft will become clearer.

Further Study

You may have noticed already that, in addition to the overall shape of the aircraft, there are two other useful aids to identification: the airline livery and the civil registration identity. These are specialist areas, which, with suitable reference books, the true civil-aviation enthusiast can positively identify not only the type of aircraft but also the individual machine, its owner/operator, and also something of its history. The section on Other Recommended Reference Sources gives details of where you can obtain these references.

INTERNATIONAL REGISTRATION PREFIX

It is possible to immediately identify the nationality of each airline operator by the first letter(s) or letter-and-number combination of its unique civil registration. This is normally carried on each side of fuselage near the tail.

Examples are G-BNWA – a Boeing 767 of British Airways; PH-AGA – an Airbus A310 of the Dutch airline KLM; NI66AA – a Douglas DC-10 of American Airlines; and 5B-DBA – an Airbus A320 of Cyprus Airways.

AP	Pakistan	HP	Panama	TC	Turkey	YV	Venezuela
A2	Botswana	HR	Honduras	TF	Iceland	Z	Zimbabwe
A3	Tonga	HS	Thailand	TG	Guatemala	ZA	Albania
A40	Oman	HV	The Vatican	TI	Costa Rica	ZK	New Zealand
A5	Bhutan	HZ	Saudi Arabia	TJ	Cameroon	ZP	Paraguay
A6	United Arab Emirates	H4	Solomon Islands	TL	Central African Republic	Z3	Macedonia
A7	Qatar	I	Italy	TN	Congo Brazzaville	3A	Monaco
A9C	Bahrain	JA	Japan	TR	Gabon	3B	Mauritius
B	China (Peoples	JY	Jordan	TS	Tunisia	3C	Equatorial Guinea
	Republic of; Taiwan)	J2	Djibouti	TT	Chad	3D	Swaziland
C/CF	Canada	J3	Grenada	TU	Ivory Coast	3X	Guinea
CC	Chile	J5	Guinea Bissau	TY	Benin	4K	Azerbaijan
CN	Morocco	J6	St Lucia	TZ	Mali	4L	Georgia
CP	Bolivia	J7	Dominica	T2	Tuvalu	4R	Sri Lanka
CS	Portugal	J8	St Vincent & Grenadines	T3	Kiribati	4U	United Nations
CU	Cuba	LN	Norway	T7	San Marino	4X	Israel
CX	Uruguay	LV	Argentina	UK	Uzbekistan	5A	Libya
C2	Nauru	LX	Luxembourg	UN	Kazakhstan	5B	Cyprus
C3	Andorra	LY	Lithuania	UR	Ukraine	5H	Tanzania
C5	Gambia	LZ	Bulgaria	VH	Australia	5N	Nigeria
C6	Bahamas	MT	Mongolia	VN	Vietnam	5R	Madagascar
C9	Mozambique	N	USA	VP-F	Falkland Islands	5T	Mauritania
D	Germany	OB	Peru	VP-LA	Anguilla	5U	Niger
DQ	Fiji	OD	Lebanon	VP-LM	Montserrat	5V	Togo
D2	Angola	OE	Austria	VP-LV	British Virgin Islands	5W	Western Samoa
D4	Cape Verde Islands	OH	Finland	VQ-T	Turks & Caicos Islands	5X	Uganda
D6	Comoro Islands	OK	Czechia	VR-B	Bermuda	5Y	Kenya
EC	Spain	OM	Slovakia	VR-C	Cayman Islands	60	Somalia
EI	Eire	OO	Belgium	VR-G	Gibraltar	6V	Senegal
EK	Armenia	OY	Denmark	VR-H	Hong-Kong	6Y	Jamaica
EL	Liberia	P	Korea (DPRK)	VT	India	70	Yemen
EP	Iran	PH	Netherlands	V2	Antigua & Barbuda	7P	Lesotho
ER	Moldova	PJ	Netherlands Antilles	V3	Belize	7Q	Malawi
ES	Estonia	PK	Indonesia	V4	St Kitts-Nevis	7T	Algeria
ET	Ethiopia	PP/PT	Brazil	V5	Namibia	8P	Barbados
EW	Belarus	PZ	Surinam	V7	Marshall Islands	8Q	Maldives
EX	Kyrgyzstan	P2	Papua New Guinea	V8	Brunei	8R	Guyana
EY	Tajikistan	P4	Aruba	XA/XB/XC	Mexico	9A	Croatia
EZ	Turkmenistan	RA	Russia	XT	Burkina Faso	9G	Ghana
E3	Eritrea	RDPL	Laos	XU	Kampuchea	9H	Malta
F	France	RP	Philippines	XY	Myanmar	9J	Zambia
G	Great Britain	SE	Sweden	YA	Afghanistan	9K	Kuwait
HA	Hungary	SP	Poland	YI	Iraq	9L	Sierra Leone
HB	Switzerland &	ST	Sudan	YJ	Vanuatu	9M	Malaysia
	Liechtenstein	SU	Egypt	YK	Syria	9N	Nepal
HC	Ecuador	SX	Greece	YL	Latvia	9Q	Zaire
HH	Haiti	S2	Bangladesh	YN	Nicaragua	9U	Burundi
HI	Dominican Republic	S5	Slovenia	YR	Romania	9V	Singapore
HK	Colombia	S7	Seychelles	YS	El Salvador	9XR	Rwanda
HL	Republic of Korea	S9	Sao Tome	YU	Yugoslavia	9Y	Trinidad & Tobago

TWO PROPELLER ENGINES – LOW WING

BEECHCRAFT 99/1900

Short-range commuter airliner

Country of Origin: United States of America

Data for 1900D Series

Engines: Two 1,280 shp (955 kW) Pratt and Whitney Canada PT6A-67 D turboprops

Dimensions:

Wingspan: 57 ft 11 in (17.65 m)

Length: 57 ft 11 in (17.65 m)

Passenger Capacity: 19

Maximum Range: 1,725 miles (2,776 km)

Maximum Cruising Speed: 332 mph (533 km/h)

History

Beechcraft's re-entry into the regional airliner market, the 1900 was developed from the King Air corporate transport and first flew in 1982. The first production version, the Model 1900C entered service in February 1984 and more than 200 were sold before production changed in 1991 to the improved 1900D. This version featured a deeper fuselage giving greater headroom and more powerful engines.

The Model 1900 can be easily distinguished from earlier, smaller, Model 99 by its "T" tail and its oval, rather than square, windows

Mesa Airlines, which acts a feeder service to the United Airlines network, is the largest user of the 1900D with a total of 118 in service and on order.

BRITISH AEROSPACE 748

Short-range regional airliner

Country of Origin: United Kingdom

Data for 748 Series 2B
Engines: Two 2,080 shp (1,982 kW) Rolls-Royce Dart RDa 7
Mark 552 turboprops
Dimensions:
Wingspan: 102 ft 6 in (31.23 m)
Length: 67 ft 0 in (20.42 m)
Passenger Capacity: 48 to 52
Maximum Range: 1,900 miles (3,055 km)
Maximum Cruising Speed: 282 mph (454 km/h)

History
Designed as a potential replacement for the
ubiquitous Douglas DC-3. Production started
in 1961 as the Hawker Siddeley 748, Series I.
Only 18 Series I were built before being
replaced by the improved Series 2 with
more powerful engines and later with an
increased wingspan.

When Hawker Siddeley became part of
British Aerospace, production continued until
1988 when a total 382 of the 748s had been
built, including 89 assembled by Hindustan
Aeronautics Limited in India.

BRITISH AEROSPACE ATP

Medium-range regional airliner

Country of Origin: United Kingdom

Data for ATP
Engines: Two 2,653 shp (1,978 kW) Pratt and Whitney
Canada PW 126A turboprops
Dimensions:
Wingspan: 100 ft 6 in (30.63 m)
Length: 85 ft 4 in (26.0 m)
Passenger Capacity: 64 to 72 – dependent upon class seating
layout
Maximum Range: 2,142 miles (3,444 km)
Maximum Cruising Speed: 306 mph (493 km/h)

History
Derived from the earlier British Aerospace
748, the ATP (advanced turboprop) airliner
was built at the same Manchester factory. The
design is some 18 feet (5.49 m) longer than its
predecessor and the engines are fitted with
advanced six-bladed propellers for increased
efficiency and noise reduction.

Following a first flight in August 1986, the
ATP entered service in May 1988. It was
renamed Jetstream 61 in 1994, and marketing
of the design stopped in 1996 with 67 built,
when the Aero International (Regional)
consortium was formed.

BRITISH AEROSPACE JETSTREAM 31/41

Short-range commuter airliner

Country of Origin: United Kingdom

Data for Jetstream 31
Engines: Two 940 shp (701 kW) Garrett TPE 331-10 UF turboprops
Dimensions:
Wingspan: 52 ft 0 in (15.85 m)
Length: 47 ft 2 in (14.37 m)
Passenger Capacity: 9 to 19 – dependent upon class seating layout
Maximum Range: 1,226 miles (1,975 km)
Maximum Cruising Speed: 303 mph (488 km/h)

History

The very successful Jetstream 31 was derived from the Handley Page HP 137 Jetstream which first flew in 1967. The financial collapse of the Handley Page company in 1969 led to production being transferred to Scottish Aviation, which in 1977 became part of British Aerospace.

Early versions powered by two Turboméca Astazou engines were delivered to the Royal Air Force but an order from the US Air Force was canceled, following the collapse of Handley Page.

The design proved to be very popular with commuter airlines in the United States, providing linking services to the major hub airports. Almost 400 Jetstream 31s have been built and since 1992 over 60 of the improved Jetstream 41s, with a maximum passenger capacity of 29, have been delivered.

CONVAIR CV 580/CV 600

Medium-range airliner

Country of Origin: United States of America

Data for Convair CV 580

Engines: Two 3,750 shp (2,800 kW) Allison 501- D31H turboprops

Dimensions:

Wingspan: 105 ft 4 in (31.12 m)

Length: 80 ft 6 in (24.84 m)

Passenger Capacity: 56

Maximum Range: 2,967 miles (4,773 km)

Maximum Cruising Speed: 342 mph (550 km/h)

History

Many of the successful series of Convair piston-engined airliners have been converted to turboprop engines. The first such modification was made by Convair in 1950 but the majority were undertaken by Pac Aero of California from the early 1960s. A total of 170 CV 340 and CV 440 airliners were fitted with the Allison 501 turboprops to become the CV 580.

Convair eventually used the Rolls-Royce Dart engines for their conversion of the CV 240 – renamed CV 600. Another version powered by the British Napier Eland turboprop were used by the Royal Canadian Air Force.

Although some 70 turboprop Convairs are still in service, most are used as cargo freighters rather than carrying passengers.

DOUGLAS DC-3

Short-range airliner

Country of Origin: United States of America

Data for DC-3:
Engines: Two 1,200 hp (896 kW) Pratt and Whitney
R–1830– 92 Twin Wasp radial piston engines
Dimensions:
Wingspan: 95 ft 0 in (28.96 m)
Length: 64 ft 6 in (19.66 m)
Passenger Capacity: 28 to 32
Maximum Range: 1,510 miles (2,430 km)
Maximum Cruising Speed: 215 mph (346 km/h)

History
Many hundreds of the venerable DC-3 remain in service worldwide, when most of the twin-turboprop airliners designed in the 1960s to replace it, are no longer in use.

The design first flew in 1935 and by the time the United States entered World War II in 1941, more than 430 were in airline service. With over 10,000 military C-47 versions built during the war, the DC–3 or Dakota (its British name) was widely available as war surplus and so became the mainstay of every postwar airline and air force.

Attempts have been made to improve and modernize the design. Douglas built a few Super DC–3s from 1949 and a number of standard DC–3s have been converted to turboprop power but most still in service retain their reliable Twin Wasp piston engines.

EMBRAER EMB-110 BANDEIRANTE (Bandit)

Short-range commuter airliner

Country of Origin: Brazil

Data for EMB– 110P2:
Engines: Two 750 shp (559 kW) Pratt and Whitney Canada PT 6A–34 turboprops
Dimensions:
Wingspan: 50 ft 3 in (15.28 m)
Length: 50 ft 4 in (15.34 m)
Passenger Capacity: 18 to 21
Maximum Range: 1,221 miles (1,964 km)
Maximum Cruising Speed: 256 mph (413 km/h)

History

When production ceased in 1990, a total of 500 Bandeirantes had been built for military and civilian customers. The most successful of the indigenous Brazilian designs, the EMB 110 was the response to a military specification for an unpressurized light transport, the first aircraft flying in 1968. The initial airliner version was the EMB-110C carrying 15 passengers, which entered service in April 1973 with the stretched P2 variant arriving in 1977.

Although no longer in production, the Bandeirante remains very popular with the smaller airlines for its reliability and good economics.

EMBRAER EMB-120 BRASILIA

Short-range regional airliner

Country of Origin: Brazil

History

Building on the success of the Bandeirante, the Brasilia was designed to carry up to 30 passengers at a greater speed and much further. Evolved from the EMB-121 Xingu pressurized business transport, the first EMB-120 entered service in October 1985. By 1991 a total of 214 had been delivered and to date more than 300 are in use throughout the Americas and Europe.

Other versions of the basic design are the extended-range EMB-120 ER and a mixed passenger/freight EMB-120 Combi and the Embraer ERJ-145 regional jet uses the same fuselage. (See Section F.)

Data for EMB-120:
Engines: Two 1,800 shp (1,343 kW) Pratt and Whitney Canada PW 118 turboprops
Dimensions:
Wingspan: 64 ft 11 in (19.78 m)
Length: 65 ft 7 in (20.00 m)
Passenger Capacity: 24 to 30
Maximum Range: 1,854 miles (2,982 km)
Maximum Cruising Speed: 343 mph (552 km/h)

FAIRCHILD METRO II/III

Short-range commuter airliner

Country of Origin: United States of America

Data for the Metro III

Engines: Two 1,000 shp (746 kW) Garrett TPE 331-11U- 612G turboprops

Dimensions:

Wingspan: 57 ft 0 in (17.37 m)

Length: 59 ft 4 in (18.09 m)

Passenger Capacity: 19

Maximum Range: 1,324 miles (2,131 km)

Maximum Cruising Speed: 320 mph (515 km/h)

History

The Metro can trace its design back to the Swearingen Merlin I/II executive transport of the early 1960s. The first Metro commuter airliner flew in 1969 and deliveries to the first customer (Air Wisconsin) began in 1973. The Metro II replaced the Metro I in production from 1975. Fairchild took over the Swearingen company and the Metro III with longer-span wings appeared in 1981.

A freighter version of the Metro III is called Expediter. The aircraft continues in production as the Metro 23 with more than 1,000 of all versions having been delivered, making the design one of the most successful commuter airliners.

ILYUSHIN IL-114

Medium-range regional airliner

Country of Origin: Russia

Data for the IL-114

Engines: Two 2,466 shp (1,840 kW) Klimov TV7–117 turboprops

Dimensions:

Wingspan: 98 ft 5 in (30.00 m)

Length: 88 ft 2 in (26.88 m)

Passenger Capacity: 60 to 68

Maximum Range: 2,982 miles (4,800 km)

Maximum Cruising Speed: 311 mph (500 km/h)

History

The design of the IL-114 was completed in 1986 but the changes within the former Soviet Union meant that the first flight did not take place until March 1990. Visually similar to the British Aerospace ATP, the Ilyushin did not enter service until the late 1990s, due in part to the crash of one of the three prototypes in 1993.

When the project was first proposed, it was anticipated that the Soviet national airline Aeroflot would require at least 500 IL-114 airliners as replacements for the Antonov AN-24. That rate of production is now much less certain.

The aircraft is assembled both in Moscow and in Tashkent (Uzbekistan) with components built in Romania, Poland, and Bulgaria. A version powered by Pratt and Whitney Canada PW 127 engines is proposed for export to western airlines.

NAMC YS-11

Short-range regional airliner

Country of Origin: Japan

Data for YS-11A-200:

Engines: Two 3,060 shp (2,280 kW) Rolls-Royce Dart 542-10K turboprops
Dimensions:
Wingspan: 105 ft 0 in (32.0 m)
Length: 86 ft 4 in (26.30 m)
Passenger Capacity: 60
Maximum Range: 1,990 miles (3,215 km)
Maximum Cruising Speed: 291 mph (470 km/h)

History

A total of 182 YS-11 airliners were built between 1962 and 1974 when production ceased. The only Japanese airliner to reach production since World War II, it was designed by Nikon Aircraft Manufacturing Company (NAMC), a consortium of a number of Japanese companies including Fuji, Kawasaki, and Mitsubishi.

Although optimized for the Japanese home market, the YS-11 nevertheless was relatively successful in North America, where operators included Piedmont Aviation and South West Airlines.

The majority of the approximately 70 YS-11s that remain in service are operated by All Nippon Airlines and Japan Air Commuter.

SAAB 340

Medium-range regional airliner

Country of Origin: Sweden

Data for Saab 340 B

Engines: Two 1,870 shp (1,399 kW) General Electric CT7-5AZ turboprops

Dimensions:

Wingspan: 70 ft 4 in (21.44 m)

Length: 64 ft 8 in (19.72 m)

Passenger Capacity: 33 to 37

Maximum Range: 2,128 miles (3,422 km)

Maximum Cruising Speed: 325 mph (522 km/h)

History

Fairchild and Saab-Scania reached agreement in January 1980 to jointly develop the Model 340 regional airliner. However, in 1985, Fairchild withdrew from the program a year after the first aircraft was delivered to the Swiss airline Crossair.

After 160 340A versions were delivered, production switched to the 340B variant which used more powerful engines and an increased span tail plane. The first 340B was delivered in September 1989.

By late 1996 over 380 Saab 340s had been delivered, justifying Saab's decision to continue the project on its own. However, with only two 340s sold in 1997, Saab announced a review of both its regional airliners and subsequently confirmed that production of the 340 will cease in 1999.

SAAB 2000

Short-range regional airliner

Country of Origin: Sweden

Data for the Saab 2000

Engines: Two 4,125 shp (3,075 kW) Allison AE 2100A turboprops
Dimensions:
Wingspan: 81 ft 3 in (24.76 m)
Length: 88 ft 8 in (27.03M)
Passenger Capacity: 50 to 58
Maximum Range: 1,890 miles (2,640 km)
Maximum Cruising Speed: 421 mph (678 km/h)

History

Fitted with six-bladed, constant-speed Dowty propellers, the Saab 2000 is claimed to be the fastest and quietest regional turboprop in production. Developed from the 340 with a stretched fuselage and increased wing span, the 2000 entered service with Crossair of Switzerland in 1994.

Production is shared between a number of European aviation companies with the tail built by Valmet in Finland, the rear fuselage by Westland in the UK, and the wing manufactured in Spain by CASA.

With a speed approaching that of the regional jets but more economical, more than 30 are now in service. However slowing of orders in 1997, led to a review of both Saab regional airliners and it was subsequently announced that production of the 2000 will cease in 1999.

25

TWO PROPELLER ENGINES – HIGH WING

AI(R) ATR42/72

Medium-range regional airliner

Countries of Origin: France and Italy

Data for ATR 42-300
Engines: Two 1,800 shp (1,342 kW) Pratt and Whitney Canada PW 120 turboprops
Dimensions:
Wingspan: 80 ft 8 in (24.57 m)
Length: 74 ft 5 in (22.67 m)
Passenger Capacity: 42 to 50
Maximum Range: 2,787 miles (4,481 km)
Maximum Cruising Speed: 309 mph (497 km/h)

History
Launched in October 1981, Avion de Transport Regional (ATR) was a joint collaborative program by Aerospatiale in France and Aeritalia (later Alenia) in Italy. The first ATR 42 to enter airline service did so in December 1985 and by early 1998 orders for over 300 had been received.

In addition to improvements of the basic ATR 42, a major stretch of the design resulted in the ATR 72. This features a 14 ft 9 in (4.5 m) longer fuselage with new outer wings and more powerful engines. Passenger capacity has been increased to a maximum of 74. The first ATR 72 entered airline service in October 1989 and at least 180 are now operating worldwide.

ATR is now part of the Aero International (Regional) group, which provides marketing and support services for ATR, Avro RJs, and Jetstream.

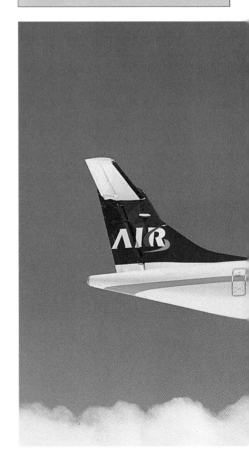

AIRTECH CN-235

Medium-range commuter airliner

Countries of Origin: Spain and Indonesia

Data for CN-235-100

Engines: Two 1,870 shp (1,395 kW) General Electric CT7-9C turboprops

Dimensions:

Wingspan: 84 ft 8 ins (25.81 m)

Length: 70 ft 1 in (21.35 m)

Passenger Capacity: 45

Maximum Range: 2,430 miles (3,910 km)

Maximum Cruising Speed: 282 mph (454 km/h)

History

Jointly designed and built by CASA of Spain and IPTN in Indonesia, the first Spanish prototype flew in November 1983 with the initial Indonesian aircraft flying a month later. Production of the components is divided between the two countries with final assembly lines in both countries.

A total of over 200 CN-235s are on order, the majority for military customers. The first civil version entered service with Merpati Nusantara in March 1988 and some 25 were in service in Spain and Indonesia 10 years later.

ANTONOV AN-24 AND XIAN Y7

Short-range regional airliner and freighter

Country of Origin: Ukraine

Data for AN-24V

Engines: Two 2,280 shp (1,887 kW) Ivchenko A1-24A turboprops

Dimensions:

Wingspan: 95 ft 10 in (29.20 m)

Length: 77 ft 3 in (23.53 m)

Passenger Capacity: 50

Maximum Range: 1,491 miles (2,400 km)

Maximum Cruising Speed: 311 mph (500 km/h)

History

The first An-24 flew in April 1963 and entered service with Aeroflot shortly after. With more than 1,100 An-24s built before Ukrainian production ceased, the type is widely used within the former Soviet bloc. The design continues to be built in China by the Xian Aircraft Manufacturing Company as the Y7.

Ukraine developments of the basic design included the AN-24RT freighter, which has a small turbojet fitted behind the right engine to improve take-off performance when heavily loaded.

It is believed that more than 800 An-24s remain in service worldwide.

CASA C-212 AVIOCAR

Short-range airliner and utility transport

Country of Origin: Spain

Data for C-212 C

Engines: Two 775 shp (580 kW) Garrett AiResearch (Now Allied Signal) TPE 331-5-251 C turboprops

Dimensions:

Wingspan: 62 ft 4 in (19.00 m)

Length: 49 ft 11 in (15.20 m)

Passenger Capacity: 22 to 26

Maximum Range: 1,044 miles (1,760 km)

Maximum Cruising Speed: 294 mph (359 km/h)

History

Conceived as a STOL (short-take-off-and-landing) replacement for the Spanish Air Force's DC-3 and Junkers JU-52 transports, the first prototype flew in March 1971.

The design's potential as a multipurpose aircraft for developing countries was soon appreciated and the first civil version was delivered in July 1975 as the C-212C. Although production of the military machines ceased in 1975 after 260 were built, development of the commercial versions have continued with improvements in engines and wing configuration giving better performance. The current production aircraft is designated C-212-300. By early 1998 a total of around 170 commercial C-212 airliners had been sold.

De HAVILLAND CANADA DHC-6 TWIN OTTER

Short-range airliner

Country of Origin: Canada

Data for Twin Otter Series 300

Engines: Two 620 shp (460 kW) Pratt and Whitney Canada PT6A-27 turboprops

Dimensions:

Wingspan: 65 ft 0 in (19.81 m)

Length: 51 ft 9 in (15.77 m)

Passenger Capacity: 20

Maximum Range: 1,059 miles (1,705 km)

Maximum Cruising Speed: 210 mph (388 km/h)

History

A worthy successor to the rugged Otter and Beaver, the Twin Otter has achieved more civil sales than either of its predecessors.

Designed for a short-take-off-and-landing performance, it first flew in May 1965, entering production as the series 100. Later series 200 and series 300 improvements had an extended nose and more powerful engines. In addition to the standard land plane, the design has frequently been used as a seaplane on floats, or with skids for use on snow.

Production ceased in 1988 after a production run of 844.

De HAVILLAND CANADA DHC-8 DASH 8

Short-range commuter airliner

Country of Origin: Canada

Data for Dash 8-100A

Engines: Two 2,000 shp (1,490 kW) Pratt and Whitney Canada PW 120A turboprops.

Dimensions:

Wingspan: 85 ft 0 in (25.91 m)

Length: 73 ft 0 in (22.25 m)

Passenger Capacity: 37 to 40

Maximum Range: 1,267 miles (2,040 km)

Maximum Cruising Speed: 305 mph (490 km/h)

History

The Dash 8 was de Havilland Canada's response to the demand in the early 1980s for a 30- to 40-seat commuter airliner. The type first flew in June 1983 and over 300 Dash 8s were in service or on order by late 1996.

The 300 series flew in 1987; improved engines and a 11 ft 3 in (3.43 m) longer fuselage increased passenger capacity to over 50. Total orders for this version exceeded 125.

The final development of the Dash 8 is the 400 series, due to enter service in 1999. This version will seat no fewer than 70 passengers.

FAIRCHILD DORNIER 228

Short-range commuter airliner

Country of Origin: Germany

Data for 228-100
Engines: Two 715 shp (535 kW) Garrett TPE331-5 turboprops
Dimensions:
Wingspan: 55 ft 7 in (16.97 m)
Length: 49 ft 3 in (15.03 m)
Passenger Capacity: 15
Maximum Range: 1,225 miles (1,970 km)
Maximum Cruising Speed: 268 mph (432 km/h)

History
The Dornier 228 evolved from the earlier Do28 and Do128 designs but was fitted with a new high-efficiency wing and better engines. The two different versions, the 100 and 200 series, were developed in parallel, the 100 giving a longer range and the 200 more passenger capacity (up to 19). Both versions first flew in 1981 and entered service the following year.

The 228 has a STOL (short-take-off-and-landing) capability and special versions can be optimized for cargo or as air ambulances with six stretchers and nine attendants as passengers.

The 200 series is also built under license in India by Hindustan Aircraft Limited, where more than 50 have been built. Total production in Germany and India is in excess of 230.

FAIRCHILD DORNIER 328

Short-range commuter airliner

Country of Origin: United States of America

Data for 328-100
Engines: Two 2,180 shp (1,627 kW) Pratt and Whitney Canada PW119B turboprops
Dimensions:
Wingspan: 68 ft 10 in (20.98 m)
Length: 69 ft 8 in (21.22 m)
Passenger Capacity: 30 to 39
Maximum Range: 1,727 miles (2,780 km)
Maximum Cruising Speed: 397 mph (640 km/h)

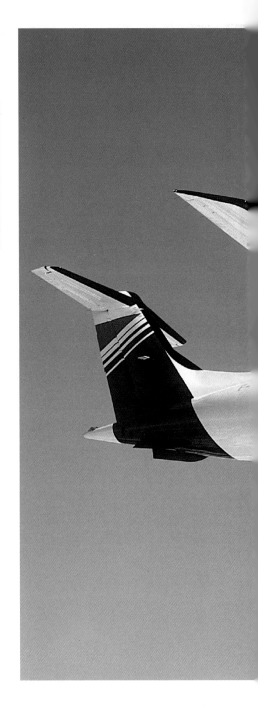

History

Designed as a very advanced follow-on from the Do228, the Do328 uses the earlier aircraft's wing but fitted to a new fuselage. The improved engines have six-bladed propellers for increased efficiency and noise reduction. The first aircraft flew in December 1991 with deliveries to customers starting in October 1993. One of the earliest customers was the American commuter airline Midway and the financial collapse of this carrier was a setback to sales of the Do328.

The Dornier Company had been part of the Deutsche Aerospace group until Fairchild purchased Dornier in 1996. The design has always had international participation with some 40 percent of the aircraft built in Korea, Italy, United Kingdom, and Israel.

After the setback caused by the failure of Midway, sales have revived and now stand at over 100, approximately half in service.

FOKKER F27/50

Short-range airliner

Country of Origin: Netherlands

Data for the F27-200

Engines: Two 2,080 shp (1,700 kW) Rolls-Royce Dart 552 Turboprops

Dimensions:

Wingspan: 95 ft 2 in (29.00 m)

Length: 77 ft 4 in (23.56 m)

Passenger Capacity: 44

Maximum Range: 1,582 miles (2,211 km)

Maximum Cruising Speed: 298 mph (480 km/h)

History

The most successful of the many so-called "Dakota Replacement" designs, the first F27 aircraft flew in November 1955. From the outset, an agreement with Fairchild led to parallel production of the design in the United States. It was a Fairchild-built aircraft that first entered service in September 1958. Development of the design also continued in parallel and the 6 ft 0 in (1.83 m) stretched version appeared first as the Fairchild FH-227 with a capacity for 52 passengers.

The F27 was destined to be built in greater numbers than any other Western turboprop – a total of 787, of which 300 remain in service.

In 1983 Fokker launched their Fokker 50 using the F27-500 fuselage with much-improved engines. At the time of the financial collapse of the Fokker Company in March 1996, orders for this version totaled over 200 – many of which are in service.

IPTN N-250

Short-range regional airliner

Country of Origin: Indonesia

Data for N-250-50

Engines: Two 3,200 shp (2,385 kW) Allison AE 2100C turboprops

Dimensions:

Wingspan: 91 ft 11 in (28.00 m)

Length: 86 ft 4 in (26.30 m)

Passenger Capacity: 50 to 54

Maximum Range: 1,267 miles (2,046 km)

Maximum Cruising Speed: 380 mph (610 km/h)

History
Since IPTN was established in the mid-1970s, due to the initiative of the Indonesian Minister of Technology, the company has steadily been increasing its technological capabilities. The N-250 is the most ambitious design to date, with the first prototype flying in August 1995. A larger N-250-100 is being offered for sale in addition to the –50 but with an increased capacity of up to 68 passengers.

Delivery of production aircraft is in progress to meet the initial orders for nearly 30 with a further 190 on option to purchase.

An agreement with General Electric has led to the establishment of the American Regional Aircraft Industry (AMRI) in Mobile, Alabama, to build the N-270 version capable of carrying up to 70 passengers.

LET L-410

Short-range commuter airliner

Country of Origin: Czech Republic

History
The design of the L-410 originated in 1966 at the Kunovice works of the Czechoslovakian LET National Corporation for use in the Soviet bloc. Initially powered by Pratt and Whitney PT6A engines, production aircraft from 1973 were fitted with M601 engines and were designation L-410M.

From 1979 the L-410 UVP version appeared with a lengthened fuselage. The current version is fitted with wing-tip fuel tanks and five-bladed propellers and designated the L-410UVP-E.

Total production of the L-410 exceeds 1,100, of which more than 500 are the UVP-E version, which continues in production.

Data for L 410 UVP-E

Engines: Two 750 shp (560 kW) Motorlet M601E turboprops

Dimensions:

Wingspan: 65 ft 7 in (19.98 m) with tip tanks

Length: 47 ft 4 in (14.42 m)

Passenger Capacity: 19

Maximum Range: 814 miles (1,318 km)

Maximum Cruising Speed: 236 mph (380 km/h)

PILATUS BRITTEN – NORMAN BN-2 ISLANDER

Short-range commuter airliner

Country of Origin: United Kingdom

Data for BN-2B

Engines: Two 300 hp (225 kW) Textron Lycoming 10 –540K flat six piston engines.
Dimensions:
Wingspan: 49 ft 0 in (14.94 m)
Length: 35 ft 8 in (10.86 m)
Passenger Capacity: 8
Maximum Range: 1,221 miles (1,965 km)
Maximum Cruising Speed: 164 mph (264 km/h)

History

This is the second design of the Isle of Wight based Britten-Norman company, and more than 1,200 Islanders have been built, making it the bestselling commercial aircraft of Western Europe.

Conceived as a replacement for the prewar de Havilland Dragon Rapide, the idea was for a strong but simple aircraft capable of operating from basic airfields. The first prototype flew in June 1965 and has been subject to steady development over the years. A turboprop version, the BN-2T, appeared in 1981 and more than 65 of this mark have been sold.

In addition to production in the United Kingdom, the design has also been built in Romania. A three-engined version called the Trislander with the third engine mounted on the tail was developed by Britten-Norman but production ceased in 1982 after 73 had been built.

SHORT 330/360

Short-range regional airliner

Country of Origin: United Kingdom

Data for 330-200

Engines: Two 1,198 shp (893 kW) Pratt and Whitney PTA-45R turboprops
Dimensions:
Wingspan: 74 ft 8 in (22.76 m)
Length: 58 ft 1 in (17.69 m)
Passenger Capacity: 30
Maximum Range: 1,054 miles (1,695 km)
Maximum Cruising Speed: 219 mph (352 km/h)

History

Derived from the successful Skyvan utility transport, the Short 330 used the same unpressurized boxlike fuselage section, but stretched to accommodate 30 passengers. The braced wing, fixed undercarriage, and twin-tail were retained, giving a somewhat antiquated appearance. The first 330 flew in July 1975 and when production ceased in 1992, a total of 136 had been sold including those for military customers.

An improved version, the 360, appeared in 1982 and was capable of carrying 36 passengers – the main visual difference was a single conventional fin. Production of this version ended in 1991 after a total of 165 had been built. Approximately 150 of the Short 330/360 remain in airline service.

SECTION B

FOUR PROPELLER ENGINES – LOW WING

DOUGLAS DC-4/6/7

Medium-to-long-range airliner

Country of Origin: United States of America

Data for DC-6
Engines: Four 1,800 hp (1,340 kW) Pratt and Whitney R-2800-CA15 Double Wasp radial piston engines.
Dimensions:
Wingspan: 117 ft 6 in (35.81 m)
Length: 100 ft 7 in (30.66 m)
Passenger Capacity: 48 to 56 dependent upon class seating layout
Maximum Range: 4,587 miles (7,376 km)
Maximum Cruising Speed: 311 mph (501 km/h)

History
The Douglas Commercial (DC) series of airliners originated with the twin-engined DC-1 of 1933. The four-engined models started with the DC-4E of 1939, which was the Douglas response to a United Airlines requirement for a long-range airliner. With the United States' entry into World War II, the DC-4 became the military C-54 and 1,162 were built for the USAAF. Although a further 78 new DC-4s were built postwar, production of the larger, faster DC-6 began in 1947. Together with military versions, a total of 665 DC-6 variants were built before production ceased in favor of the DC-7.

The last Douglas piston engined airliner, the DC-7 was also the largest and the first to be capable of non-stop London–New York transatlantic flights carrying up to 105 passengers. A total of 338 were built.

Over 200 DC-4/6/7 airliners remain in service, used as freighters or for special tasks like water bombing.

39

ILYUSHIN IL-18

Medium-range airliner

Country of Origin: Russia

Data for IL-18D

Engines: Four 3,830 shp (3,170 kW) Ivchenko A1-20M turboprops

Dimensions:

Wingspan: 122 ft 9 in (37.40 m)

Length: 117 ft 9 in (35.90 m)

Passenger Capacity: 110 to 122 dependent upon class seating layout

Maximum Range: 4,040 miles (6,500 km)

Maximum Cruising Speed: 419 mph (675 km/h)

History

The Il-18, designed in response to an Aeroflot requirement for a 75- to 100-seat medium-range airliner, first flew in July 1957 and entered service in April 1959.

A contemporary of its Western equivalents, the Lockheed Electra and the British Vickers Vanguard, the Il-18 was destined to be built in greater numbers – an estimated 600 for civilian operators plus many more for military purposes including maritime reconnaissance.

During the cold war, the Il-18 had the NATO reporting name of "Coot" and although most have now been superseded by jet equipment, it is estimated that nearly 100 remain in service on charter work.

LOCKHEED L-188 ELECTRA

Short-to-medium-range airliner

Country of Origin: United States of America

Data for L-188C

Engines: Four 3,750 shp (2,800 kW) Allison 501-D13 turboprops

Dimensions:

Wingspan: 99 ft 0 in (30.18 m)

Length: 104 ft 6 in (31.81 m)

Passenger Capacity: 104

Maximum Range: 2,510 miles (4,023 km)

Maximum Cruising Speed: 405 mph (652 km/h)

History

Although designed in response to an American Airlines requirement, the type first entered service with Eastern Airlines in January 1959. Initial prospects for the aircraft looked promising with orders for over 140 at the time of service entry, but two crashes during 1959 and a third in 1960 caused loss of confidence by the traveling public. The aircraft was not grounded, though, and following modifications the design was fully cleared by 1961. However the bad start together with the growing acceptance of jet airliners meant that total sales of the Electra were restricted to 170, of which some 50 remain in service.

VICKERS VISCOUNT

Short-range airliner

Country of Origin: United Kingdom

Data for V.810 series

Engines: Four 1,920 shp (1,566 kW) Rolls-Royce Dart 525 turboprops

Dimensions:

Wingspan: 93 ft 9 in (28.50 m)

Length: 85 ft 8 in (26.11 m)

Passenger Capacity: 69

Maximum Range: 1,010 miles (1,625 km)

Maximum Cruising Speed: 350 mph (563 km/h)

History

The world's first turboprop airliner, the Viscount entered service with British European Airlines (BEA) in April 1953, a year after the de Havilland Comet had become the world's first turbojet airliner. The Viscount attracted many sales especially in North America where its economy and smooth flight were much appreciated by both airlines and their passengers.

The initial production version, the V.700 series, carried between 47 and 60 passengers but the V.800 series were the most popular, contributing to total Viscount sales of 438 when production ceased in 1964. The Viscount thus became Britain's most successful turbine-powered airliner. Today only a handful of Viscounts remain in service, mainly as freighters.

FOUR PROPELLER ENGINES – HIGH WING

ANTONOV AN-12 and SAC Y-8

Medium-range freighter

Country of Origin: Ukraine

Data for An-12

Engines: Four 3,495 shp (2,942 kW) Ivchenko A1-20K turboprops

Dimensions:

Wingspan: 124 ft 8 in (38.00 m)

Length: 108 ft 7 in (33.10 m)

Passenger Capacity: 14 passengers and freight to 44,000 lb (20,000kg)

Maximum Range: 3,540 miles (5,700 km)

Maximum Cruising Speed: 416 mph (670 km/h)

History

The Antonov An-12 was built to meet a Soviet Air Force requirement for a military freighter. It is essentially a militarized version, with a rear-loading ramp, of the civil An-10, of which approximately 500 were manufactured.

The first An-12 flew in 1958 and some 900 were constructed by 1973, of which probably 200 saw civilian service with Aeroflot, Cubana, LOT Polish Airlines, and others.

China also chose the An-12 as its basic turboprop freighter but commissioned a redesign by the XIAN company, which resulted in the fitment of 4,250 shp (3170 kW) Zhuzhou WJ6 turboprops. The aircraft is built by the Shaanxi Aircraft Company and is in service with the Chinese Air Force and the civil CAAC airline as well as other nationalities.

De HAVILLAND CANADA DHC-7 DASH 7

Short-range, short-take-off-and-landing airliner

Country of Origin: Canada

Data forDHC-7 Series 100
Engines: Four 1,120 shp (835 kW) Pratt and Whitney PT6A-50 turboprops
Dimensions:
Wingspan: 93 ft 0 in (28.35 m)
Length: 80 ft 6 in (24.54 m)
Passenger Capacity: 54
Maximum Range: 1,347 miles (2,168 km)
Maximum Cruising Speed: 261 mph (420 km/h)

History
The Dash 7 is the largest of the de Havilland Canada's family of quiet STOL airliners and although production ended in 1988, following Boeing's acquisition of the company, its capabilities are still unrivaled.

Following the prototype's first flight in March 1975, the type entered service in February 1978 with Rocky Mountain Airways.

Variations of the basic 100 series model included the 101 which was in an all cargo version and the 150 series, which had increased fuel capacity giving a maximum range of 2,900 miles (4,680 km).

A total of 111 Dash 7s were built, of which some 75 remain in service.

LOCKHEED-MARTIN L-100 HERCULES

Medium-range freighter

Country of Origin: United States of America

Data for L-100-30

Engines: Four 4,680 shp (3,490 kW) Allison 501-D22A turboprops
Dimensions:
Wingspan: 132 ft 7 in (40.41 m)
Length: 112 ft 9 in (34.37 m)
Passenger Capacity: Payload of 51,000 lb (23,180 kg)
Maximum Range: 5,734 miles (9,227 km)
Maximum Cruising Speed: 355 mph (571 km/h)

History

The L-100 Hercules is the civilian equivalent of the legendary C-130 Hercules military freighter of which more than 2,200 have been built.

A 1951 USAF requirement for a turboprop freighter led to the Lockheed Company producing the prototype Hercules in August 1954. The first civilian version was based on the C-130E model and flew in 1965. Initial sales were slow until, in 1968, Lockheed offered the L-100-20 and later the L-100-30, which proved to be the most successful version of the 50 or so civilian Hercules now in service.

A major redesign of the military Hercules has resulted in the C-130J with new engines and cockpit avionics, which is in production for the USAF and the RAF. A civil version designated L-100J is being offered for civilian use.

TWO JET ENGINES – LOW WING

AIRBUS A300/A310

Medium-to-long-range airliner

Countries of Origin: European Consortium

Data for A300-600

Engines: Two Pratt and Whitney PW4000 or General Electric CF6-80C2 turbofans in the thrust class of 56,000 to 61,500 lbst (249-273.6 kN)

Dimensions:
Wingspan: 147 ft 1 in (44.84 m)
Length: 177 ft 5 in (54.08 m)
Passenger Capacity: 267 or freight to 121,290 lb (55,017kg)
Maximum Range: 5,873 miles (9,450 km)
Maximum Cruising Speed: 557 mph (897 km/h)

History

The A300 was the first design of the highly successful European Consortium involving Aerospatiale, CASA, British Aerospace, and Deutsche Aerospace. The first A300B1 flew in October 1972 and the initial-production A300B2 joined Air France in May 1974. It was the first wide-body, twin-jet airliner, with orders of 248 when production ceased in 1984. The improved version, called the A300-600, continues in production with over 200 on order by the mid-1990s.

The A300-600ST Super Transporter, nicknamed Beluga, is a special version featuring an oversized fuselage to carry Airbus components

The A310 was the result of a shortened fuselage, reducing passenger capacity to a maximum of 230, but with an increased range of up to 5,950 miles (9,580 km). More than 250 A310s have been sold to date.

AIRBUS A 319/A320/A321

Short-to-medium-range airliner

Countries of Origin: European Consortium

Data for A320-200

Engines: Two 25,000 lbst (111.2 kN) CFM 56-5AI or IAE V2500-A1 turbofans

Dimensions:

Wingspan: 111 ft 10 in (34.09 m)

Length: 123 ft 3 in (37.57 m)

Passenger Capacity: 150 to 179 dependent upon class seating layout

Maximum Range: 3,397 miles (5,463 km)

Maximum Cruising Speed: 561 mph (903 km/h)

History

With aerospace companies in Germany, France, Britain, Spain, and Belgium participating, the first A320 flew in February 1987. It was the second completely new Airbus design providing a narrow-body twin-jet in the 150-to-170-seat range. It was the first airliner to provide a computerized fly-by-wire control system with an advanced computerized cockpit. Also, for the first time, the central pilot control columns were replaced by side controllers.

Variations of the basic A320 include the A319 with a reduced fuselage length of 110 ft 11 in (33.8 m), carrying a maximum of 142 passengers, and the A321, with a 146 ft (44.50 m) fuselage capable of holding 220 passengers.

Orders for the A319/A320/A321 family total over 1,000 with more than 600 already in service.

AIRBUS A330

Medium-to-long-range wide-body airliner

Country of Origin: European Consortium

Data for A 330-300

Engines: Two General Electric CF6-80 E1 or Pratt and Whitney PW 4000 or Rolls-Royce Trent turbofans in the thrust class 64,000 to 67,000 lbst (284 to 304.6 kN)

Dimensions:

Wingspan: 197 ft 8 in (60.3 m)

Length: 208 ft 10 in (63.65 m)

Passenger Capacity: 295 to 440 dependent upon class seating layout

Maximum Range: 5,585 miles (8,950 km)

Maximum Cruising Speed: 547 mph (880 km/h)

History

The twin-engined Airbus 330 was launched in June 1987, simultaneously with the four-engined A340, the only significant difference being in the number of engines installed.

The A330 is the largest of Airbus's twin-jet family and flew for the first time in November 1992 with service entry at the end of 1993. It shares the advanced features initiated by the A320, i.e. side sticks and fly-by-wire flight controls. It is also the first Airbus to offer a Rolls-Royce engine as an alternative to the General Electric and Pratt and Whitney power plants. Cathay Pacific were the launch customers for the Rolls-Royce Trent-engined A330.

Orders for over 140 A330s have been placed with some 50 in service to date. As with the A320, Airbus Industrie are offering variations on the theme. The A330-200 series with a passenger capacity of 293 has a range of up to 7,370 miles (11,850 km). Orders for over 30 have been placed, with first deliveries in 1998.

BOEING 737

Short-to-medium-range airliner

Country of Origin: United States of America

Data for 737-300
Engines: Two CFM International CFM56-3B turbofans in the thrust range 20,000 to 22,000 lbst (88.97 to 97.9 kN)
Dimensions: Wingspan: 94 ft 9 in (28.88 m)
              Length: 109 ft 7 in (33.40 m)
Passenger Capacity: 128 to 149 dependent upon class seating layout
Maximum Range: 3,091 miles (4,973 km)
Maximum Cruising Speed: 565 mph (908 km/h)

History

Since the Boeing 737 first entered service in February 1968, it has become the world's most successful jet airliner with total sales of all versions reaching 3,500. The initial 100 and 200 series versions can be easily distinguished from the later aircraft by their slim, small-diameter Pratt and Whitney JT8D engines. Although production of the 200 series ended in 1988 after 1,144 were built, well over 900 remain in service.

The 300 series launched the new 737 family into service in November 1984 and sales of this version are fast approaching those of the 200 series. The 400 series can offer a passenger capacity of up to 188, whereas the 500 is optimized for short-range operation.

Finally, Boeing have launched their Next Generation 737-600/700/800 series and already secured orders for over 500.

BOEING 757

Medium-range narrow-body airliner

Country of Origin: United States of America

Data for 757-200

Engines: Two Rolls-Royce RB211-535 turbofans in the 37,400 to 40,100 lbst (166.4 to 178.4 kN) thrust range or two Pratt and Whitney PW 2000 turbofans in the 38,200 to 41,700 lbst (170 to 185.5 kN) thrust range

Dimensions: Wingspan: 124 ft 10 in (38.05 m)

Length: 155 ft 3 in (47.32 m)

Passenger Capacity: 178 to 239 dependent on class seating layout

Maximum Range: 4,606 miles (7,410 km)

Maximum Cruising Speed: 568 mph (914 km/h)

History

After a prolonged assessment of the design to replace the Boeing 727, the 757 project was launched in March 1979. The design used the same fuselage diameter as the first generation of Boeing jets (707, 727, and 737) but was much longer with a new wing and turbofan engines.

The 757 first entered service with Eastern Airlines on 1 January 1983. Initially orders were slow to come but since the late 1980s the 757 has become one of Boeing's bestsellers with over 850 ordered.

In September 1996 the 300 series was announced for delivery in 1999 with a 23 ft 4 in (7.1 m) longer fuselage to give increased passenger capacity.

BOEING 767

Medium-to-long-range wide-body airliner

Country of Origin: United States of America

History

Developed in parallel with the 757, the wide-body 767 has the same two-crew flight deck but is otherwise of a totally different design. Announced in July 1978, the 757 reached airline service in September 1982, when United Airlines received their first JT9D-powered version.

An-extended range model, the 767-200ER version of the 200 series has proved the most popular. The success of the 767 encouraged Boeing to stretch the fuselage by 21 ft 1 in (6.42 m) and offer the Rolls-Royce RB 211-524 in the 767-300.

Total orders of the 767 exceed 1,200, the majority of which are now in service.

Data for 767-200

Engines: Two Pratt and Whitney JT9D or two Pratt and Whitney PW 4050 or two General Electric CF6-80C turbofans in the 48,000 to 52,500 lbst (213.5 to 233.5 kN) thrust range

Dimensions: Wingspan: 156 ft 1 in (47.57 m)

Length: 159 ft 2 in (48.51 m)

Passenger Capacity: 216 to 290 dependent upon class seating layout

Maximum Range: 4,433 miles (7,135 km)

Maximum Cruising Speed: 571 mph (914 km/h)

BOEING 777

Medium-to-long-range wide-body airliner

Country of Origin: United States of America

Data for 777-200

Engines: Two Pratt and Whitney PW 4074 or two General Electric GE90-75B or two Rolls-Royce Trent 875 turbofans in the 74,000 to 75,000 lbst (332 to 336 kN) thrust range.

Dimensions:

Wingspan: 196 ft 11 in (60.02 m)

Length: 209 ft 1 in (63.73 m)

Passenger Capacity: 305 to 440 dependent upon class seating layout

Maximum Range: 4,836 miles (7,778 km)

Maximum Cruising Speed: 564 mph (905 km/h)

History

Initially conceived as a stretched 767 and designated 767-X, the aircraft was finally launched in October 1990, as a completely new design, fitting in size between the 767-300 and the 747-400.

Like other airliners in its class, the 777 is expected to be offered in a family of variants covering medium-to-long-range with differing fuselage lengths. A wide choice of large turbofan engines is also being offered from the big three aero-engine manufacturers.

The 777 is the first Boeing airliner to have fly-by-wire linked to an advanced computerized cockpit. It is currently being offered in three versions: the Series 200; the Series 200 IGW (Increased Gross Weight) with range up to 8,500 miles (13,670 km); and the series 300. The last, with engines up to 100,000 lbst (445 kN), will be the world's largest twin-jet and – at 242 ft 4 in (73.86 m) – the longest. Orders for all 777 versions are near 350.

TUPOLEV Tu-204

Medium-range narrow-body airliner

Country of Origin: Russia

Data for 204-200
Engines: Two 35,580 lbst (158.3 kN) Aviadvigatel PS-90A turbofans
Dimensions:
Wingspan: 137 ft 10 in (42.00 m)
Length: 150 ft 11 in (46.00 m)
Passenger Capacity: 190–214 dependent upon class seating layout
Maximum Range: 3,932 miles (6,330 km)
Maximum Cruising Speed: 530 mph (850 km/h)

History
Russia's most advanced airliner, the Tu-204 was originally designed to meet an Aeroflot requirement for a replacement of the Tri-jet Tu-154. Fitted with specially developed turbofan engines, fly-by-wire digital flight controls, with analogue back up, the Tu-204 is the Russian counterpart to the Boeing 757.

Following a first flight in January 1989, small numbers of the aircraft are now in service in Russia.

To broaden the appeal of the aircraft in the Western market, Tupolev are now offering the Tu- 204-220 with two 43,100 lbst (191.7 kN) Rolls-Royce RB 211-535 E4 turbofans and Rockwell Collins avionics. The Kato Group of Egypt has ordered 13 of this version.

Other versions of the 204 being promoted are the 214, which is a combination freighter and passenger carrier, the 224 with 166 seats and Rolls-Royce engines, and the similar-sized 234 with PS-90 engines.

TWO JET ENGINES – TAIL-MOUNTED

BOMBARDIER CANADAIR REGIONAL JET

Regional airliner

Country of Origin: Canada

Data for CRJ-100

Engines: Two 9,220 lbst (41.0 kN) General Electric CF34-3A turbofans

Dimensions:

Wingspan: 69 ft 7 in (21.21 m)

Length: 87 ft 10 in (26.77 m)

Passenger Capacity: 50 to 52

Maximum Range: 2,188 miles (3,520 km)

Maximum Cruising Speed: 529 mph (851 km/h)

History

The Canadair Regional Jet was derived from the Canadair CL601 Challenger corporate jet transport by lengthening the fuselage 20 ft (6.1 m) and increasing the wing area. The design was the first in a completely new class of 50-seat airliners offering the speed of the larger jets but with costs, over the longer ranges, comparable to the faster turboprops.

The first CRJ flew in May 1991 and has sold well, with more than 170 orders by 1998. The largest operator in the USA is Comair, based in Cincinnati, which operates a fleet of 45 CRJ-100s.

A further development, the CRJ-700 – stretched to give a passenger capacity of 70 – is also being offered to airlines.

BRITISH AEROSPACE ONE-ELEVEN

Short-range jet airliner

Country of Origin: United Kingdom

Data for One-Eleven Series 500

Engines: Two 12,550 lbst (55.8 kN) Rolls-Royce Spey MK 512-14DW turbofans

Dimensions:

Wingspan: 93 ft 6 in (28.50 m)

Length: 107 ft 0 in (32.61 m)

Passenger Capacity: 119

Maximum Range: 2,165 miles (3,484 km)

Maximum Cruising Speed: 541 mph (870 km/h)

History

The British Aircraft Corporation BAC 111, as it was then known, was launched in May 1961 with an order for 10 from the independent British United Airways. Following a first flight in August 1963, entry into service took nearly two years due in part to the loss of one prototype and its test crew. This accident was caused by a phenomenon unique to rear-engined T-tail aircraft called "the deep stall," from which the aircraft could not be recovered.

The initial version was the One-Eleven-200, followed by the 300 and 400 series operating at higher weights. The 500 series featured a stretched fuselage, increased-span wings, and more powerful engines, and has been the most successful version of the One-Eleven.

A total of 232 aircraft were built in the United Kingdom until production was transferred to Romania, who are building a version powered by the Rolls-Royce Tay 650 with 15,100 lbst (67.2 kN) called the Airstar 2500.

EMBRAER ERJ-145

Regional airliner

Country of Origin: Brazil

Data for ERJ-145
Engines: Two 7,040 lbst (31.3 kN) Allison AE 3007A turbofans
Dimensions:
Wingspan: 65 ft 9 in (20.4 m)
Length: 98 ft 0 in (29.87 m)
Passenger Capacity: 50
Maximum Range: 1,600 miles (2,575 km)
Maximum Cruising Speed: 495 mph (797 km/h)

History

The ERJ-145 was originally known as the EMB-145, and its development has, unlike that of its immediate competitor, the Bombardier-Canadair RJ, been somewhat protracted and difficult.

The initial concept announced in 1989 was a jet adaptation of the EMB-120 Brasilia with 75 percent of the structure being the same. The engines were to be mounted forward of the wing with the jet efflux passing over the wings. However, wind-tunnel testing revealed that this engine installation was unsuitable and by 1991 the current configuration was chosen.

This hiatus meant that the first flight was delayed to August 1995 but this did not prevent a major order, announced at the September 1996 Farnborough Air Show in England, from Continental Express of Houston, Texas.

A 37-seat variant, the ERJ-135, and a larger ERJ-170 carrying up to 70 passengers are also available.

FOKKER F28/F70/F100

Short-range regional airliner

Country of Origin: Netherlands

Data for F28-4000 Fellowship

Engines: Two 9,900 lbst (44.3 kN) Rolls-Royce RB 183-2 MK 555 turbofans

Dimensions:

Wingspan: 82 ft 3 in (25.07 m)

Length: 97 ft 2 in (29.61 m)

Passenger Capacity: 85

Maximum Range: 1,295 miles (2,085 km)

Maximum Cruising Speed: 502 mph (808 km/h)

History

The F28 Fellowship was designed to complement the very successful F27 Friendship and first flew in May 1967. The German airline LTU received the first production aircraft in February 1969 with the longer-fuselage 4000 variant flying in October 1976.

Sales of civil and military F28s reached 241 to more than 50 operators when production ceased in 1986 in favor of the Fokker 100. Based on the F28 but with a stretched fuselage having a passenger capacity of 122, and more efficient Rolls-Royce Tay turbofans, the F100 was immediately successful. Swissair received the first delivery in February 1988 and orders for nearly 300 had been received when the Fokker Company collapsed financially in 1996.

The shortened-fuselage F70 variant had attracted some 50 orders prior to 1996.

McDONNELL DOUGLAS DC-9/MD-80/MD-90

Short-to-medium-range airliner

Country of Origin: United States of America

Data for MD-87
Engines: Two 20,000 lbst (88.9 kN) Pratt and Whitney JT8D-217C turbofans
Dimensions:
Wingspan: 107 ft 10 in (32.86 m)
Length: 130 ft 5 in (39.7 m)
Passenger Capacity: 130
Maximum Range: 3,262 miles (5,246 km)
Maximum Cruising Speed: 576 mph (925 km/h)

History

Originating in the 80-seat DC-9-10, which entered service in December 1965, this family of twin-engined airliners have undergone more changes and development than any other airliner in history. From the DC-9-10 with two 12,250 lbst (54.5 kN) engines and a fuselage 104 ft 5 in (31.82) long, the design has evolved into the MD-90 with engines twice as powerful – 25,000 lbst (111.2 kN) – and a fuselage length of 152 ft 7 in (46.51 m), capable of carrying 187 passengers. That's more than twice as many as its "tiny" predecessor.

In over 30 years, more than 2,440 DC-9s and its derivatives have been sold. The MD-95 version remains in production as the Boeing 717.

TUPOLEV Tu-134

Short-range airliner

Country of Origin: Russia

Data for Tu-134A
Engines: Two 14,990 lbst (66.7 kN) Soloviev D-30 Series II turbofans
Dimensions:
Wingspan: 95 ft 2 in (29.00 m)
Length: 121 ft 7 in (37.05 m)
Passenger Capacity: 84
Maximum Range: 1,877 miles (3,020 km)
Maximum Cruising Speed: 560 mph (898 km/h)

History

A contemporary of its Western equivalents, the BAC One-Eleven and the Douglas DC-9, the Tu-134 also shared the rear-engined T-tail configuration. It was the third of the Tupolev design bureau's commercial aircraft. Development of the type was rather protracted with five years between the start of flight testing in 1962 and entry into Aeroflot service in September 1967.

The improved Tu-134A featured a 6 ft 11 in (2.10 m) fuselage stretch and more powerful engines.

It is estimated that over 700 Tu-134s were built, of which some 170 were exported and over 400 remain in service.

THREE JET ENGINES – LOW WING AND TAIL-MOUNTED

LOCKHEED L-1011 TRISTAR

Medium-to-long-range wide-body airliner

Country of Origin: United States of America

Data for L-1011-500
Engines: Three 50,000 lbst (222.4 kN) Rolls-Royce RB211-524B turbofans
Dimensions:
Wingspan: 164 ft 4 in (50.09 m)
Length: 164 ft 3 in (50.05 m)
Passenger Capacity: 330
Maximum Range: 6,998 miles (11,260 km)
Maximum Cruising Speed: 596 mph (960 km/h)

History

The last in the long line of Lockheed airliners, the L-1011 Tristar was designed and built in direct competition with Douglas DC-10. Whereas the Douglas aircraft used an American engine, the Tristar was the first to use the new, very advanced, Rolls-Royce RB211 three-shaft turbofan. Shortly after the Tristar's first flight in November 1970, the cost of developing the RB211 caused the bankruptcy of Rolls-Royce. Although Rolls-Royce was, in effect, eventually nationalized and the RB211 safeguarded, many early potential Tristar sales were lost to its rival.

The L-1011-1 entered service with Eastern Airlines in April 1972. The later L-1011-100 and L-1011-200 had up-rated engines and could accommodate up to 400 passengers. The last variant, the L-1011-500, had a reduced-length fuselage to give maximum range.

A total of 250 Tristars were built before production ceased in 1984 and approximately 160 remain in service.

McDONNELL DOUGLAS DC-10/MD-11

Medium-to-long-range wide-body airliner

Country of Origin: United States of America

Data for MD-11

Engines: Three 61,500 lbst (273.6 kN) General Electric CF6-80C2 or three 60,000 lbst (266.9 kN) Pratt and Whitney PW4460 turbofans

Dimensions:

Wingspan: 169 ft 6 in (51.70 m)

Length: 200 ft 10 in (61.21 m)

Passenger Capacity: 323 to 405 dependent upon class seating layout

Maximum Range: 9,480 miles (15,250 km)

Maximum Cruising Speed: 587 mph (945 km/h)

History

Designed in competition with the Lockheed Tristar to meet an American Airlines requirement, the Douglas DC-10/McDonnell Douglas MD-11 has been the more successful, despite early major setbacks.

Entering service in August 1971 with both American Airlines and United Airlines as the medium-range DC-10-10, it was followed by the larger range DC-10-30 for European customers in 1973. The type suffered a number of disastrous accidents in the mid-1970s, including what was then the world's worst, when a Turkish Airlines DC-10 crashed near Paris. However, the causes were identified and overcome, and production continued until 1989 when a total of 386 commercial DC-10s plus 60 KC-10A military tankers had been built.

The MD-11 was launched in 1986 as a successor to the DC-10 and the first entered service in December 1990. Although it was available in advance of its Airbus A330 and Boeing 777 competitors, sales have been slow with total orders around 170 at the time of writing, of which some 150 are in service.

THREE JET ENGINES – TAIL-MOUNTED

BOEING 727

Short-to-medium-range airliner

Country of Origin: United States of America

Data for 727-200

Engines: Two Pratt and Whitney JT8D turbofans in various thrust ratings from 14,500 lbst (64.4 kN) to 17,400 lbst (77.3 kN)

Dimensions:

Wingspan: 108 ft 0 in (32.92 m)

Length: 153 ft 2 in (46.69 m)

Passenger Capacity: 189

Maximum Range: 2,764 miles (9,447 km)

Maximum Cruising Speed: 610 mph (982 km/h)

History

The first-production 727-100 entered service with Eastern Airlines in February 1963 and was capable of carrying a maximum of 131 passengers. The stretched 200 series followed into service in December 1967 with Northeast Airlines. The fuselage had been lengthened by 10 ft (3.05 m) but otherwise, technically, the two versions were identical.

The need to increase the fuel capacity and hence range of the 200 series led to the Advanced 727-200, which flew for the first time in March 1972. This variant was the bestselling version until production ended in 1984.

In the 20-plus years the 727 was in production a total of 1,831 were sold and over 900 remain in service. Because of present noise regulations, which the standard JT8D engines cannot meet, manufacturers are offering a number of special noise-reduction measures or re-engining the 727 with more modern engines.

TUPOLEV TU-154

Medium-range airliner

Country of Origin: Russia

Data for TU-154M

Engines: Three 23,380 lbst (104 kN) Soloviev D-30KU-154 turbofans

Dimensions:

Wingspan: 123 ft 3 in (37.55 m)

Length: 157 ft 2 in (47.90 m)

Passenger Capacity: 180

Maximum Range: 4,103 miles (6,600 km)

Maximum Cruising Speed: 591 mph (950 km/h)

 3

History

The TU-154 flew in October 1968 with the first delivery to the Soviet Union's national airline, Aeroflot, in 1971. Initially powered by three 20,950 lbst (93.9 kN) Kuznetsov engines, the early TU-154s could carry a maximum of 167 passengers.

Designed to replace the first Tupolev jet, the TU-104, but with the ability to operate from remote airfields with gravel runways, the TU-154 had a multi-wheeled undercarriage and a good short-field performance.

The improved TU-154M was fitted with quieter and more economical Soloviev (now Aviadvigatel) engines and remains in production, although, as the TU-204 becomes more accepted, it is likely to be phased out of production.

It is believed that some 900 TU-154s have been built with at least 750 remaining in service.

YAKOVLEV YAK-40

Short-range regional airliner

Country of Origin: Russia

Data for YAK-40
Engines: Three 3,300 lbst (14.7 kN) Ivchenko AI-25 turbofans
Dimensions:
Wingspan: 82 ft 0 in (25.00 m)
Length: 66 ft 10 in (20.36 m)
Passenger Capacity: 27 to 32
Maximum Range: 1,118 miles (1,800 km)
Maximum Cruising Speed: 342 mph (550 km/h)

History
The first Yakovlev jet airliner, the YAK-40 was designed to replace a range of piston-engined airliners including the Li-2, which were the licensed-built Douglas DC-3s.

The first prototype flew in October 1966 and total production, which is now complete, was approximately 1,000, the majority of which were delivered to Aeroflot.

The tri-jet configuration and unswept wing were chosen to give a good short-field performance at remote airfields. Built-in ventral air stairs and an auxiliary power unit to start the engines were also installed.

YAKOVLEV YAK-42

Short-range airliner

Country of Origin: Russia

Data for YAK-42
Engines: Three 14,330 lbst (63.74 kN) Lotarev (now Progress) D-36 turbofans
Dimensions:
Wingspan: 114 ft 5 in (34.88 m)
Length: 119 ft 4 in (36.38 m)
Passenger Capacity: 96 to 120 dependent upon class seating layout
Maximum Range: 1,180 miles (1,900 km)
Maximum Cruising Speed: 503 mph (810 km/h)

History
Designed for similar operating conditions to the earlier YAK-40, the YAK-42 retains the same tri-jet configuration. An integral auxiliary power unit (APU) for ground power, engine starting, and air-conditioning – together with built-in air stairs – facilitates operation independent of ground services at remote airfields.

Comparable in size with the early DC-9 and Boeing 737, the YAK-42 entered service with Aeroflot in 1980.

An improved version the YAK-42D is capable of an increased range of up to 1,365 miles (2,200 km) and a number have been exported to China and Cuba. Total production of the YAK-42 is believed to be more than 270.

FOUR JET ENGINES – LOW WING

AIRBUS 340

Very-long-range wide-body airliner

Countries of Origin: European Consortium

Data for A340-200

Engines: Four 31,200 lbst (140 kN) CFM International CFM56-5C-2 turbofans

Dimensions:

Wingspan: 197 ft 8 in (60.3 m)

Length: 194 ft 10 in (59.39 m)

Passenger Capacity: 263 to 303 dependent on class seating layout

Maximum Range: 9,212 mile (14,800 km)

Maximum Cruising Speed: 568 mph (914 km/h)

History

Launched simultaneously with the A330, the two designs have the same cockpit instruments, fuselage and wings, the number of engines being the most significant visual difference. Optimized for long-range, the choice of four engines on the A-340 provides the most fuel-economic solution.

The A340-300 uses the same fuselage length as the A330 and provides accommodation for up to 335 passengers. The very-long-range version, the A340-200, has a reduced-length fuselage, trading additional passengers for fuel.

The first A340 to enter airline service did so with Lufthansa and Air France in March 1993 and a total of over 140 were on order by 1996.

Developments of the A340 are being offered to the airlines with ranges of over 9,500 miles (15,400 km), carrying 315 passengers.

BOEING 707

Long-range airliner

Country of Origin: United States of America

Data for 707-320B

Engines: Four 18,000 lbst (80 kN) Pratt and Whitney JT3D-3 Turbofans

Dimensions:

Wingspan: 145 ft 9 in (44.42 m)

Length: 152 ft 11 in (45.60 m)

Passenger Capacity: 147 to 219 dependent upon class seating layout

Maximum Range: 5,758 miles (9,265 km)

Maximum Cruising Speed: 605 mph (973 km/h)

History

It was the Boeing 707 that transformed the world airliner market by offering a combination of speed, range, capacity, and comfort level that no other aircraft in the 1960s could match.

The 707 was a great commercial success and ensured that Boeing airliners would have world dominance for 30 years. However, it was a $16 million gamble by the company to build the model 367-80 prototype that made it all possible. From that early aircraft, which flew in 1954, both the 707 and the military KC-135 Stratotanker were developed.

Pan American introduced the 707-120 into service in December 1957 and a series of versions with different engines and fuselage lengths were built up to 1978, when production ceased. Of the 878 manufactured, some 120 remain in commercial use, the majority as freighters, although noise regulations are increasingly restricting the operation of the unmodified aircraft.

BOEING 747

Long-range wide-body airliner

Country of Origin: United States of America

Data for 747-400

Engines: Four Pratt and Whitney PW 4000 or four General Electric CF6 –80C or four Rolls-Royce RB211-524 in the 56,750 lbst (252.39 kN) to 58,000 lbst (258 kN) thrust range.

Dimensions:

Wingspan: 211 ft 5 in (64.44 m)

Length: 231 ft 10 in (70.66 m)

Passenger Capacity: 412 to 660 dependent upon class seating layout

Maximum Range: 8,325 miles (13,390 km)

Maximum Cruising Speed: 584 mph (939 km/h)

History

If the 707 created the conditions that made possible Boeing's dominance of the world airline market, it was the 747 that confirmed it. Its size permitted massive reductions in operating costs and, more than with any other aircraft, created the present world air travel market.

Pan-American was again the first airline to operate this revolutionary Boeing aircraft in January 1970. As with its 707 predecessor, the basic design evolved to meet differing airline requirements. A special longer-range model, the 747SP, had the fuselage shortened by 47 ft 1 in (14.35 m) to give a maximum range of 9,575 miles (15,400 km), but with a reduced passenger capacity. The major development of the 747 was the 400 series, which offered more powerful engines, a new two-crew cockpit, and increased range. Since 1990 this has been the standard 747 version.

Sales of the 747 now exceed 1,250, almost equally divided between the early 100 and 200 series models and the improved 300 and 400 series. Most remain in service.

ILYUSHIN IL-86/IL-96

Medium-to-long-range wide-body airliner

Country of Origin: Russia

Data for IL-96M

Engines: Four 37,000 lbst (164.6 kN) Pratt and Whitney PW 2337 turbofans

Dimensions:

Wingspan: 197 ft 3 in (60.11 m)

Length: 209 ft 9 in (63.94 m)

Passenger Capacity: 312 to 375 dependent upon class seating layout

Maximum Range: 7,139 miles (11,500 km)

Maximum Cruising Speed: 541 mph (870 km/h)

History

The IL-96M is the latest version of Russia's wide-body airliner and with its American engines and two-crew advanced cockpit, is a determined effort to achieve sales to Western airlines.

The first wide-body airliner built in the former Soviet Union was the IL-86, which entered service with Aeroflot in 1980 after a rather protracted development. Although a total of 103 were built and most remain in service with Russian and other CIS airlines, the aircraft failed to fulfill its potential, mainly due to high operating costs.

A major redesign produced the IL-96, which in its 300 version offers fly-by-wire controls, computer cockpit, and advanced wing aerodynamics. The IL-96-300 entered service in 1993 with Aeroflot Russian International Airlines.

McDONNELL DOUGLAS DC-8

Medium-to-long-range airliner

Country of Origin: United States of America

Data for DC-8 Super 70

Engines: Four 22,000 lbst (97.9 kN) CFM International 56-2-C5 turbofans

Dimensions:

Wingspan: 148 ft 5 in (45.20 m)

Length: 187 ft 5 in (57.10 m)

Passenger Capacity: 269

Maximum Range: 5,562 miles (8,950 km)

Maximum Cruising Speed: 552 mph (888 km/h)

History

The Super 70 was the last variant of the DC-8 family of airliners, being a re-engining of the Super 60 series to give better fuel economy and increased range.

The DC-8 was the first Douglas jet airliner but the prototype did not fly until 1958, when the Boeing 707 was about to enter airline service. Despite the previous dominance of the Douglas in the airline market, it was never able to overcome the sales advantage that the 707 had gained.

The first DC-8-10s were, like the early 707s operated wit⁀   United Sates. It was the series ?⁀   ⸱⸱ intercontinental range, t⁀   ⸱⸱ificant overseas sales. The major redevelopment of the DC-8 was the 60 series, which with a 36 ft 8 in (11.18 m) fuselage stretch increased passenger capacity from a previous maximum of 179. This version entered airline service in February 1967 and, when DC-8 production finished in May 1972, a total of 262 Super 60s had been built. The earlier shorter-fuselage models had achieved total sales of 295. Around 250 DC-8s remain in service.

FOUR JET ENGINES – HIGH WING

A I (R) AVRO RJ / BAe 146

Short-range regional airliner

Country of Origin: United Kingdom

Data for BAe 146-200
Engines: Four 6,970 lbst (31.1 kN) Textron Lycoming ALF 502R-5 turbofans
Dimensions:
Wingspan: 86 ft 0 in (26.21 m)
Length: 93 ft 10 in (28.60 m)
Passenger Capacity: 85 to 112 dependent upon class seating layout
Maximum Range: 1,865 miles (2,910 km)
Cruising Speed: 477 mph (767 km/h)

History
The BAe 146 was conceived by the de Havilland design team of the Hawker Siddeley Group in 1973, but financial considerations delayed production until the creation of British Aerospace. The prototype flew for the first time in September 1981.

The BAe 146 broke new ground with its low external noise levels, which permitted jet operations at airports where noise restrictions had previously excluded jets.

From the initial 100 series, which achieved 34 sales including three VIP versions to the Royal Air Force, the design passed through 200 and 300 series versions with increasing passenger capacity.

In 1990, British Aerospace revamped the 146 family recognizing that "Regional Jet" was the marketing term that sold aircraft of the 146 class. Also, the Avro name was resurrected to prefix the RJ70, RJ85, RJ100, and RJ115 designations, which indicated the passenger seating capacity. Sales of the 146/RJ family have exceeded 320 and continue as part of the A I (R) consortium.

ANTONOV AN-124 RUSLAN

Long-range heavy-lift freighter

Country of Origin: Ukraine

Data for AN-124

Engines: Four 51,590 lbst (229.5 kN) Lotarev (now Progress) D-18T turbofans

Dimensions:

Wingspan: 240 ft 6 in (73.30 m)

Length: 226 ft 9 in (69.60 m)

Passenger Capacity: 88 and freight to a maximum payload of 330,700 lb (150,000kg)

Maximum Range: 10,248 miles (16,500 km)

Maximum Cruising Speed: 539 mph (865 km/h)

History

The first AN-124 flew in December 1982 and for many years was the world's largest aircraft. Commercial use of the AN-124 began in January 1986. The aircraft has set a succession of payload records including the heaviest single load – a power generator and platform weighing 291,940 lb, (132.4 tonnes)

The aircraft has nose and tail cargo doors, permitting easy loading of heavy and outsized loads. The maximum weight of the AN-124 of 892,875 lb (405 tonnes) is spread over a 24-wheel undercarriage.

Approximately 60 AN-124s have been built and most are flown by military operators.

ILYUSHIN IL-76

Medium-to-long-range heavy freighter

Country of Origin: Russia

Data for IL-76T

Engines: Four 26,455 lbst(117.7 kN) Aviadvigatel D-30KP turbofans

Dimensions:

Wingspan: 165 ft 8 in (50.50 m)

Length: 152 ft 10 in (46.59 m)

Passenger Capacity: Maximum payload 88,185 lb (40,000kg)

Maximum Range: 4,163 miles (6,700 km)

Maximum Cruising Speed: 530 mph (850 km/h)

History

The IL-76 has been a most successful heavy-lift freighter with more than 800 in service.

Following a first flight in 1971, the type entered civilian service in 1975. Like most military freighters, the IL-76 is designed to operate from unprepared airstrips with its gross weight of 418,875 lb (190 tonnes) spread over a 20-wheel undercarriage, including a nose unit fitted with four low-pressure tires. Developments of the design include the IL-76TD which has a maximum payload of 110,230 lb (50 tonnes).

FOUR JET ENGINES – TAIL-MOUNTED

ILYUSHIN IL-62

Long-range airliner

Country of Origin: Russia

Data for IL-62M

Engines: Four 24,250 lbst (107.9 kN) Soloviev D-30KU turbofans

Dimensions:

Wingspan: 141 ft 9 in (43.20 m)

Length: 174 ft 4 in (53.12 m)

Passenger Capacity: 174

Maximum Range: 6,218 miles (10,000 km)

Maximum Cruising Speed: 560 mph (900 km/h)

History

Visually similar to the contemporary British VC-10 (now operated only by the Royal Air Force), the IL-62 was the Soviet Union's first jet airliner capable of long-range intercontinental flights.

Although the prototype flew in January 1963, the first long-range service (from Moscow to Montreal) was not flown until September 1967. The improved IL-62M flew in 1971 and provided more economical engines and increased fuel capacity. The final version, the IL-62 MK, is capable of carrying a maximum of 195 passengers.

Although manufacturing ceased in 1994 after a production run of 250 aircraft, over 160 remain in service with Aeroflot Russian International Airlines and other former Soviet bloc airlines.

SECTION L

FOUR JET ENGINES – DELTA

AEROSPATIALE/BRITISH AEROSPACE CONCORDE

Medium-range supersonic airliner

Countries of Origin: France and United Kingdom

Data for Concorde

Engines: Four 38,050 lbst (169.1 kN) Rolls-Royce/SNECMA Olympus 593 Mk 610 reheated turbojets

Dimensions:

Wingspan: 83 ft 10 in (25.56 m)

Length: 203 ft 9 in (62.17 m)

Passenger Capacity: 128 to 144 dependent on class seating layout

Maximum Range: 4,088 miles (6,580 km)

Maximum Cruising Speed: 1,354 mph (2,179 km/h)

History

Although a technical triumph, Concorde proved to be an economic disaster for the British and French governments, who paid the high cost of its development.

Design studies for a supersonic airliner made independently in France and Britain resulted in very similar designs, leading to an agreement in 1962 to produce what became known as Concorde.

Advanced engineering solutions were adopted to solve the problems of sustained supersonic flight. Military aircraft, even today, do not fly supersonically for long periods. Manufacture was divided between the two countries with components delivered to duplicated assembly lines in France and Britain.

The French prototype was the first to fly, in March 1969, followed by a further three test aircraft. A protracted development program meant that service entry was not until January 1976. Of the 14 production aircraft, 13 remain in service with British Airways and Air France.

AERO-ENGINES

Although aerodynamic and constructional improvements have played a significant role in the development of commercial aircraft, it is the aero-engine that has been the dominant factor in creating the worldwide air travel we know today.

The design of the reciprocating piston engine reached a peak in the mid 1940s, just as the first turbojet turbine engines were being produced. Although piston engines are still the normal choice for small aircraft, today their use in airliners is largely restricted to the survivors of the 1940s and 1950s. It is the turbine engine that, in its various forms, provides the power for the world's commercial aircraft.

a) THE TURBINE AERO-ENGINE

The Turbojet. The first turbine engines were pure turbojets in which all the air entering the engine passed through the combustion chamber to be expanded and ejected as thrust. The early turbojets were much more powerful than the piston engines that they began to replace but at the cost of greater fuel consumption. The penalty for high speed was short-range. The turbojet's other major advantage over the piston engine was its relative technical simplicity. Far fewer moving parts meant much greater reliability, longer operating life, and reduced vibration. Very few pure turbojets remain in service, largely because of their high noise levels, but also because of their poor fuel economy.

The Turboprop. The first adaptation of the turbojet was the turboprop. In this the central shaft of the turbine is extended forward to couple to a gearbox and to drive a propeller. This gave significantly better fuel economy than the turbojet – albeit at a reduced maximum speed – but retained much of the turbojet's simplicity and smoothness. The first commercial aircraft to use the turboprop was the Vickers Viscount. Although some higher-powered turboprops were developed, today the modern turboprop is almost universally used in medium-sized aircraft.

The Turbofan. This concept evolved in the 1960s and can best be described as a combination of the turbojet and the turboprop. In the turbofan, the "propeller," much reduced in diameter, is enclosed within the engine casing. It was initially called the bypass engine because the air from the front fan (propeller) bypasses the rest of the engine interior, especially the combustion area. Early turbofans were defined as having a bypass ratio of, say, 1:1, in which as much air is bypassed as passes through the "core" of the engine. The present size of the very large turbofan engines is mainly due to the diameter of the front fan, which gives a bypass ratio of 6:1 or even more. That means six times as much air is bypassed as passes through the engine.

b) AERO-ENGINE POWER

The power rating of the aero-engine is defined in differing terms dependent upon the type of engine. The piston engine is still rated in horsepower (hp) or kilowatts (kW), the turboprop is usually given in shaft horsepower (shp) or again kilowatts (kW). Both the turbojet and turbofan are measured in pounds static thrust (lbst) or kilonewtons (kN).

The way in which the power output of the engine has controlled the development of the jet airliner can best be understood by the following examples:

i) de Havilland Comet 1

The four engines of the world's first jet airliner, the de Havilland Comet 1 of 1950 (no longer in service) each gave a maximum thrust of 5,000 lbst (22.25 kN). Total installed thrust equalled 20,000 lbst (89 kN).

ii) Boeing 707

The Boeing 707 (1957) also had four engines, each with a thrust of 17,000 lbst (76.2 kN). Total installed thrust equalled 68,000 lbst (304.8 kN).

iii) Lockheed Tristar

The first Lockheed Tristar of 1972 had three engines each producing 42,000 lbst (187 kN). Total installed thrust equalled 168,000 lbst (748 kN).

iv) Boeing 777-300

The latest Boeing 777-300 is powered by just two engines, each having an output of up to 100,000 lbst. (445 kN). Total installed thrust equalled 200,000 lbst (890 kN).

	De Havilland Comet 1	Boeing 777-300
Date:	1950	1998
Number of Engines:	Four	Two
Total installed Thrust:	20,000 lbst (89 kN)	200,000 lbst (890 kN)
Maximum number of Passengers:	44	550
Maximum range:	1,750 miles (2,816 km)	6,500 miles (10,460 km)

A tenfold increase in installed power with immeasurably better fuel consumption, permitting the carriage of more than ten times the number of passengers nearly four times as far!

C) THE AERO-ENGINE MANUFACTURERS

As the cost of developing a new aero-engine has dramatically increased, so the number of separate aero-engine manufacturers has been drastically reduced by amalgamation and takeover. Also many international collaboration agreements, sharing the cost of development, have been concluded.

i) United Kingdom. In the mid 1950s there were nine separate aero-engine manufacturers. Now, in effect, Rolls-Royce is the sole survivor (despite its financial collapse in 1971). Rolls-Royce also has a number of collaborative agreements with both European and American companies. For example the International Aero Engine AG (IAE) with its headquarters in Connecticut, which produces the IAE V2500 for the Airbus A319/A320/A321 family. The partners in IAE include Rolls-Royce, Pratt and Whitney, Japanese Aero Engine, MTU of Germany, and Fiat Avio of Italy.

ii) United States of America. The major aero-engine manufacturers in the USA are:

- Allison – based in Indianapolis – manufactures a range of turboprop and helicopter engines. Allison is now part of the Rolls-Royce group of companies.

- Garrett – with its headquarters in Phoenix, Arizona – makes smaller turbofans mainly for executive jets.

- General Electric – located in Ohio, second only to Pratt and Whitney in size – produces a range of aero-engines covering every application from airliner to fighter.

- Pratt and Whitney – with its headquarters at East Hartford, Connecticut – is the world's largest producer of gas turbine engines. By the early 1990s Pratt and Whitney had delivered 68,000 aviation turbine aero-engines, of which more than 27,000 were for commercial use.

- Textron Lycoming – based in Stratford, Connecticut – is best known for its wide range of light piston engines but also makes a number of turbofan and turboshaft engines for executive aircraft and helicopters.

iii) Russia and the Ukraine. Most of the familiar names from the former Soviet era have now disappeared with the break-up of the USSR, but the following are some of their successors.

- "Aviadvigatel" – more correctly PNPP "Aviadvigatel" which in full is Perm Scientific and Production Enterprise "Aircraft Engines." Based in Perm, Russia, the company was founded in 1939 under the Shvetsov name but known as Soloviev from 1953. Engines are produced for civil and military applications, including helicopters.

- Klimov Corporation – located in St Petersburg, formerly Leningrad – is one of the few companies still trading under their original names. Its turbojet experience dates back to 1946 when it built a copy of the Rolls-Royce Nene as the Klimov VK-1, the powerplant of the famous MiG-15.

- ZMDB Progress – a Ukraine State Enterprise. The initials mean Zaporozhye Machine-Building Design Bureau. When founded in 1945, the company was known as Ivchenko, but in 1960 it became Lotarev. A total in excess of 30,000 ZMDB Progress gas-turbine aero-engines have been built powering a wide range of military and civil aircraft.

BIBLIOGRAPHY

Air Britain Publications	*Airline Fleets 1997* *UK and Ireland Civil Aircraft Registers 1997*
Andrews C.F.	*Vickers Aircraft Since 1908* (1969 London UK)
Bowers Peter M	*Boeing Aircraft Since 1916*, 2nd Edition (1989 London UK)
Francillon René J	*Lockheed Aircraft Since 1913*, 2nd Edition (1987 London UK)
Frawley Gerard	*International Directory of Civil Aircraft* (1997 Shrewsbury UK)
Green William & Swanborough Gordon	*Observers Airliners* (1991 London UK) *Observers Aircraft* (1992 London UK)
Gunston Bill	*World Encyclopaedia of Aero Engines* (1986 Letchworth UK) *Rolls-Royce Aero engines* (1989 Frome UK)
Lambert Mark	*Jane's All the Worlds Aircraft 1992-93* (1992 Coulsdon UK)

OTHER RECOMMENDED REFERENCE SOURCES

Air Britain Civil Registers	Available from Air Britain Sales Dept 5 Bradley Road, Upper Norwood, London, SE19 3NT, England.
Ian Allan Publications	Available from Ian Allan Mail Order Dept ABA 15, 10–14 Eldon Way, Lineside Estate, Littlehampton, West Sussex, BN17 7HE, England.

Aeroflot	8
Aerospatiale/British Aerospace Concorde	74
AI(R) ATR42/72	26-27
AI(R) Avro RJ	70
Airbus	9
Airbus A300/310	45
Airbus A319/320/321	46-47
Airbus A330	48
Airbus A340	64
Airtech CN-235	28
Antonov AN-12	42
Antonov AN-24	28
Antonov AN-124 Ruslan	71
Antonov SAC Y-8	42
Beechcraft 99/1900	12
Boeing	9
Boeing 707	65, 77
Boeing 727	60-61
Boeing 737	49
Boeing 747	66-67
Boeing 757	50
Boeing 777	51, 77
Bombardia Canadair	53
Braniff	8
British Aerospace one-eleven	54
British Aerospace 146	70
British Aerospace 748	13
British Aerospace ATP	13
British Aerospace Concorde 74	74
British Aerospace Jetstream 31/41	14-15
Casa C-212 Aviocar	29
Concorde	74
Convair CV 580/600	16
De Havilland Comet	77
De Havilland Dash 7	43
De Havilland Dash 8	30
De Havilland Twin Otter	30
Douglas DC-3	17
Douglas DC-4/6/7	39
Eastern Airlines	8
Embraer EMB-110 Bandeirante	18
Embraer EMB-120 Brasilia	19
Embraer ERJ-145	55
Fairchild Dornier 228	31
Fairchild Dornier 328	32-33
Fairchild Metro II/III	20-21
Fokker F27/50	34
Fokker F28/70/100	56
Go	8
Ilyushin IL-18	40
Ilyushin IL-62	72-73
Ilyushin IL-76	71
Ilyushin IL-86/96	68
Ilyushin IL-114	22
IPTN N-250	35
LET L-410	35
Lockheed L-188 Electra	40
Lockheed-Martin L-100 Hercules	44
Lockheed Tristar 58	77
McDonnell Douglas	8
McDonnell Douglas DC-8	69
McDonnell Douglas DC-9/MD-80/MD-90	57
McDonnell Douglas DC-10/MD-11	59
NAMC YS-11	23
Pan-American	8
Pilatus Britten-Norman BN-2 Islander	36-37
SAAB	9
SAAB 340	24
SAAB 2000	25
Short 330/360	38
Tupolev Tu-134	57
Tupolev Tu-154	62
Tupolev Tu-204	52
Turbofan	76
Turbojet	76
Turboprop	76
Valujet	8
Vickers Viscount	41
VLCT	9
Xian Y7	28
Yakovlev YAK-40	63

INDEX

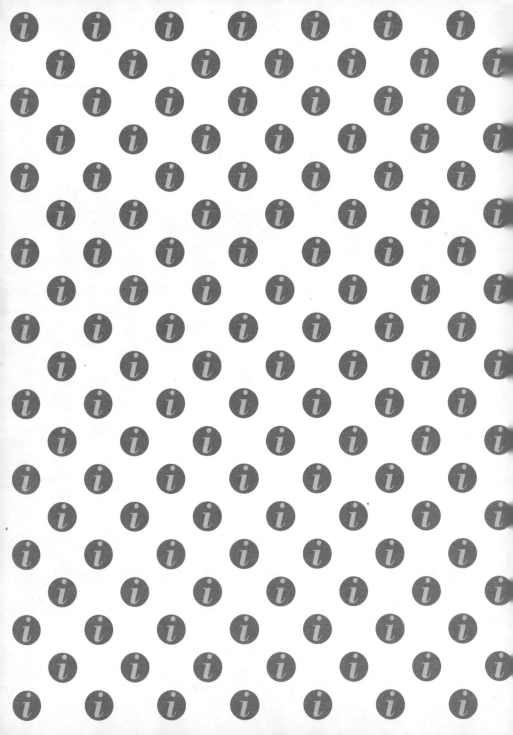